WNBA Hot Ticket

NEW YORK LIBERTY

JOSH ANDERSON

Lerner Publications ◆ Minneapolis

The stats and information in this book are accurate through August 2024.

Copyright © 2025 by Lerner Publishing Group, Inc.

All rights reserved. International copyright secured. No part of this book may be reproduced, stored in a retrieval system, or transmitted in any form or by any means—electronic, mechanical, photocopying, recording, or otherwise—without the prior written permission of Lerner Publishing Group, Inc., except for the inclusion of brief quotations in an acknowledged review.

Lerner Publications Company
An imprint of Lerner Publishing Group, Inc.
241 First Avenue North
Minneapolis, MN 55401 USA

For reading levels and more information, look up this title at www.lernerbooks.com.

Main body text set in Aptifer Slab LT Pro / Typeface provided by Linotype AG

Library of Congress Cataloging-in-Publication Data

Names: Anderson, Josh, author.
Title: New York Liberty / Josh Anderson.
Description: Minneapolis, MN : Lerner Publications, [2025] | Series: WNBA hot ticket (Lerner sports) | Includes bibliographical references and index. | Audience: Ages 7–11 | Audience: Grades 2–3 | Summary: "With stars Breanna Stewart and Sabrina Ionescu, the New York Liberty are one of the hottest teams in the WNBA. Explore the team's history and find out why their future has never looked so bright"—Provided by publisher.
Identifiers: LCCN 2024030469 (print) | LCCN 2024030470 (ebook) | ISBN 9798765669716 (library binding) | ISBN 9798765669969 (paperback) | ISBN 9798765669983 (epub)
Subjects: LCSH: New York Liberty (Basketball team)—Juvenile literature. | Women's National Basketball Association—Juvenile literature. | Women basketball players—United States—Juvenile literature.
Classification: LCC GV885.52.N44 A53 2025 (print) | LCC GV885.52.N44 (ebook) | DDC 796.323/6409747—dc23/eng/20230702

LC record available at https://lccn.loc.gov/2024030469
LC ebook record available at https://lccn.loc.gov/2024030470

Manufactured in the United States of America
1 – CG – 12/15/24

TABLE OF CONTENTS

LEADING LIBERTY 4

FACTS AT A GLANCE 5

CHAPTER 1
NEW YORK STATE OF MIND 9

CHAPTER 2
AMAZING STARS 15

CHAPTER 3
THE SHOT 21

CHAPTER 4
A BRIGHT FUTURE 27

Glossary 30
Learn More 31
Index 32

Breanna Stewart (*left*) shoots over the Connecticut Sun's Alyssa Thomas during the 2023 WNBA Playoffs.

LEADING LIBERTY

FACTS AT A GLANCE

- In 2023, the New York Liberty played in their first **WOMEN'S NATIONAL BASKETBALL ASSOCIATION (WNBA) FINALS** in more than 20 years.

- The **LIBERTY** were one of the WNBA's best teams during the league's early years. They played in four of the first six WNBA Finals.

- The Liberty picked future star **SABRINA IONESCU** in the 2020 WNBA Draft after winning only 10 games during the 2019 season.

- **TERESA WEATHERSPOON'S** half-court shot in the 1999 WNBA Finals was chosen by ESPN as the top play in league history.

It was the New York Liberty's biggest game in more than 20 years. The team was one win from the 2023 WNBA Finals. They had been ahead for most of the second half of Game 4 against the Connecticut Sun. But with less than three minutes to go in the game, a free throw put Connecticut ahead 75–74.

The Liberty's star point guard, Courtney Vandersloot, dribbled up the court. Vandersloot dribbled near teammate Breanna Stewart

Stewart blocked Vandersloot's defender. Then Stewart moved up and stood right outside the three-point line. The play left Stewart wide open.

Vandersloot spotted Stewart and fired a pass to her. Stewart jumped and took a three-point shot. The ball swished through the net, giving the Liberty a 77–75 lead. New York would never trail again on its way to the team's first Finals appearance since 2002.

After every WNBA season, some players whose contracts have ended become free agents. Free agents can join a different team. The best free agent before the 2023 season was Breanna Stewart, who had played her entire career for the Seattle Storm. The five-time All-Star had been named the league's Most Valuable Player (MVP) in 2018. She won the award again in 2023, a few weeks after leading the Liberty to the Finals against the Las Vegas Aces. Although the Liberty lost in the Finals, fans in New York were thrilled to have one of the best players in the league taking the floor for their team.

Courtney Vandersloot (*left*) dribbles past a Connecticut Sun defender during the 2023 WNBA Playoffs.

Breanna Stewart averaged 18.4 points and 10.2 total rebounds per game during the 2023 WNBA Playoffs.

Sabrina Ionescu (*left*) and Courtney Vandersloot (*right*) celebrate an overtime win in 2023.

CHAPTER 1
NEW YORK STATE OF MIND

The New York Liberty were one of the original eight teams to play in the WNBA during the league's first season in 1997. Named for New York City's Statue of Liberty, the team played many of its early years at Madison Square Garden. The Garden is nicknamed the World's Most Famous Arena. It is also home to the National Basketball Association's (NBA) New York Knicks.

The Liberty played most of their games at Madison Square Garden in New York City until 2017.

The Liberty were one of the league's most successful teams in the WNBA's early years. Behind future Basketball Hall of Fame players Teresa Weatherspoon and Rebecca Lobo, the Liberty earned a spot in the first WNBA Finals. Although they lost to the Houston Comets, the Liberty continued to find great success.

The Liberty played in the WNBA Finals three more times in their early years. But each time, New York came up empty. The Liberty lost twice more in the Finals to the Houston Comets and once to the Los Angeles Sparks. It would be more than 20 years before the team made the Finals again.

Rebecca Lobo (*center left*) played for two other WBNA teams after her four seasons with the Liberty.

In July 2024, 17,758 fans came to Barclays Center to watch the Liberty play the Chicago Sky, setting an all-time attendance record for the Liberty.

Before the Liberty made the 2023 WNBA Finals, the team went through their least successful period. The Liberty missed the playoffs from 2018 to 2020. New York won only 10 games in 2019 and two in 2020. But during the 2020 WNBA Draft, the Liberty picked University of Oregon star Sabrina Ionescu. Ionescu would become an All-Star player in New York.

In 2019, the Liberty were sold to the owner of the NBA's Brooklyn Nets. In 2021, the Liberty began playing in Barclays Center in Brooklyn, New York, where the Nets also play. Even with losing records in 2021 and 2022, the Liberty managed to make the playoffs each season before losing in the first round.

HOOPS SCOOP

Liberty guard Teresa Weatherspoon was the WNBA's first assists leader. In 1997, she averaged 6.2 assists per game.

Jonquel Jones played six seasons with the Connecticut Sun before joining the Liberty in 2023.

To help improve ahead of the 2023 season, the Liberty added superstar Breanna Stewart. Then the team traded for another former MVP, four-time All-Star center Jonquel Jones. The team also added five-time All-Star point guard Courtney Vandersloot.

With so many star players, the Liberty were on track to face the league's other top team, the Las Vegas Aces. Although the Aces got the better of New York in the 2023 Finals, the Liberty returned with all of their stars for 2024. Fans of the team hope the Liberty's first WNBA title is right around the corner.

HER TIME TO PLAY

At the start of the 2024 season, the Liberty held an event for more than 50 girls in the New York City area. At the Her Time to Play event, girls got to watch the Liberty practice, ask questions of coaches and players, and take part in basketball drills with the team on the Barclays Center court. The goal was to encourage young girls to play basketball and build interest in women's sports.

Programs such as Her Time to Play allow athletes to make a difference off the court and improve their community.

Many incredible athletes have played for the Liberty since the team's first season in 1997.

CHAPTER 2
AMAZING STARS

Hall of Fame guard Teresa Weatherspoon was a team leader from 1997 to 2003. She helped bring the Liberty to four WNBA Finals and won the WNBA's Defensive Player of the Year award twice. She was an All-Star player five times in her career. Weatherspoon's career average of 5.3 assists per game ranks sixth in WNBA history.

Teresa Weatherspoon (*center*) scored 1,247 points in her seven seasons with the Liberty.

Although she set records in college at Colorado State, guard Becky Hammon was not picked in the 1999 WNBA Draft. She joined the Liberty and served as Weatherspoon's backup for Hammon's first few seasons. As she gained playing time, Hammon became a top player in the league, earning six All-Star selections. After her playing career, she became the first full-time assistant coach in the NBA. She then went on to coach the WNBA's Las Vegas Aces.

After she retired from playing and before she became a coach in the WNBA, Becky Hammon was only the second woman to coach in the NBA.

Tina Charles (*right*) grabs a rebound in a 2018 game against the Atlanta Dream.

Center Tina Charles played for the Liberty from 2014 to 2019. During that time, she was a five-time All-Star and the 2012 WNBA MVP. She finished in the top three for MVP voting four more times. Charles ranks second in WNBA history with more than 3,800 rebounds for her career. She ranks third in scoring, and she's one of only five players in league history with more than 7,000 points.

The Liberty selected Sabrina Ionescu in the 2020 WNBA Draft. Ionescu set the all-time college basketball record for most triple-doubles while at the University of Oregon and gave the Liberty a player to build around. The 5-foot-11 (1.8 m) guard has been a WNBA All-Star three times. She has averaged more than 16 points, five rebounds, and five assists for her career.

While her history with the Liberty only began in 2023, Breanna Stewart made an impact right away in New York when she led the team to the 2023 WNBA Finals. Stewart has twice won the league's MVP award and has been picked as an All-Star player six times. With Stewart on the Liberty's roster, the team has a good chance of competing in the playoffs for a WNBA title.

In 2024, Sabrina Ionescu became just the seventh Liberty player to score 2,000 career points.

HOOPS SCOOP

When Breanna Stewart won the 2023 WNBA MVP award, she became the first Liberty player to earn that honor.

Liberty forward Sue Wicks (*right*) blocks a shot from Comets player Sonja Henning during the 1999 WNBA Finals.

CHAPTER 3
THE SHOT

The greatest play in the history of the New York Liberty may be the greatest play in the history of the entire league. Playing in the team's second WNBA Finals in 1999, the Liberty lost Game 1 in New York City. They would need to win Game 2 in Houston, Texas, to stay alive and force a winner-take-all Game 3 against the Comets.

Sophia Witherspoon takes the ball to the basket against a Comets defender. Witherspoon spent three seasons with the Liberty.

With 2.4 seconds left in Game 2, Houston's Tina Thompson hit a shot to put the Comets up 67–65. With very little time remaining, the Liberty needed to move the ball down the entire length of the court. Liberty center Kym Hampton threw the ball in to Teresa Weatherspoon. Weatherspoon dribbled up the court quickly with time running out.

The clock was about to expire before Weatherspoon could even reach the half-court line. So Weatherspoon leaped and hurled the ball in the direction of the basket. It was the kind of shot that, even for a pro, almost never goes in.

Kym Hampton (*left*) was on the first Liberty roster in 1997. She was the team's starting center for three years before an injury forced her to retire.

After her successful WNBA career, Teresa Weatherspoon (*right*) became the head coach of the WBNA's Chicago Sky in 2024.

The ball hung in the air, hit the backboard, and bounced through the net. The Liberty won the game 68–67, keeping their title hopes alive on Weatherspoon's amazing shot. WNBA fans will always remember the incredible play. The shot was chosen by ESPN as the top WNBA play of all time.

HOOPS SCOOP

Tina Charles is the Liberty's all-time leader in points and rebounds.

Almost 25 years later, the Liberty faced the Washington Mystics in the first round of the 2023 WNBA Playoffs. After the Liberty won the first game by 15 points, Game 2 was more of a battle. The Mystics led by six with less than four minutes to play. But the Liberty battled back to send the game to overtime.

The game stayed close through the overtime. With 11 seconds left, Breanna Stewart hit two free throws to give the Liberty a three-point lead. They added two more points, also from Stewart, for a 90–85 overtime victory. The win sent the Liberty into the next round of the playoffs before losing to the Aces in the Finals.

Jonquel Jones averaged 17 points and 11.6 total rebounds for the Liberty during the 2023 WNBA Playoffs.

Breanna Stewart (*right*) has won two WNBA championships and three Olympic gold medals. In her first season with the Liberty, Stewart averaged 23 points per game.

CHAPTER 4
A BRIGHT FUTURE

After years of trailing behind men's basketball with fans, women's hoops and the WNBA are on the rise. Some of that is due to Indiana Fever superstar Caitlin Clark. In 2024, she set the all-time college scoring record at the University of Iowa. Her many fans followed her to the WNBA. But Clark is only one of many exciting and talented players in the league.

The Fever's Caitlin Clark (*left*) and the Liberty's Kayla Thornton (*right*) fight for the ball during a 2024 game.

After shrinking from a high of 16 teams in the early 2000s, the league had 12 teams in 2024. But in 2025, the league will expand for the first time in over a decade. One new team will play in Northern California in the same arena as the NBA's Golden State Warriors. Another team will begin play in Toronto, Ontario, Canada, in 2026.

After the longest stretch of losing seasons in team history from 2018 to 2022, the Liberty rose again to become one of the league's top teams. Breanna Stewart is an MVP candidate every season she takes the court. Jonquel Jones is a former MVP herself. She can dominate the game from the center position. In 2023, Courtney Vandersloot moved up to second on the all-time WNBA assists list. And Sabrina Ionescu continues to improve her game, helping the team in a variety of ways.

Liberty coach Sandy Brondello led the Phoenix Mercury to the WNBA title in 2014. She knows how to win big games. The question is whether she can put all of her star pieces together and give New York its first WNBA crown.

Sandy Brondello (*center*) coached the Phoenix Mercury for eight seasons before taking over the Liberty in 2022.

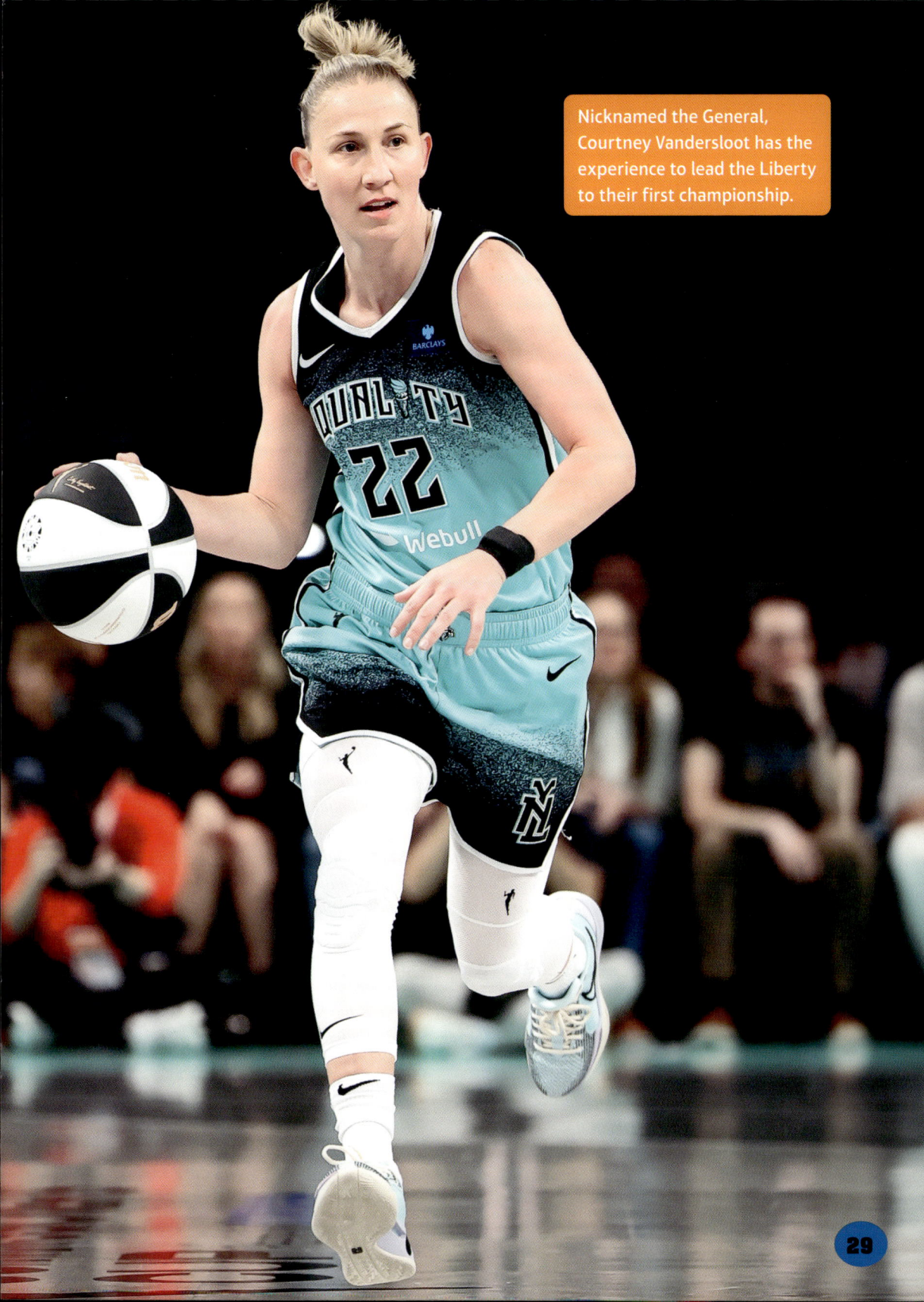

Nicknamed the General, Courtney Vandersloot has the experience to lead the Liberty to their first championship.

GLOSSARY

All-Star: one of the best players in a sports league. Each season, WNBA All-Stars play in the All-Star Game.

assist: a pass that leads directly to a basket

Basketball Hall of Fame: a museum in Springfield, Massachusetts, that honors the best basketball players and coaches

draft: when teams take turns choosing new players

free throw: an open shot taken from behind a set line after a foul by an opponent

overtime: an extra period played at the end of a game that is tied

playoffs: games held after the season to determine each year's champion

rebound: grabbing and controlling the ball after a missed shot

roster: a list of players on a team

triple-double: when a player reaches at least 10 in three different stats categories in a game

WNBA Finals: a series of games played to decide the season's champion

LEARN MORE

Goldstein, Margaret J. *Meet Sabrina Ionescu*. Minneapolis: Lerner Publications, 2024.

Leed, Percy. *Basketball's NBA and WNBA Finals*. Minneapolis: Lerner Publications, 2025.

New York Liberty
https://liberty.wnba.com/

Whiting, Jim. *The Story of the New York Liberty*. Mankato, MN: Creative Education and Creative Paperbacks, 2024.

WNBA
https://www.wnba.com/

Women's National Basketball Association Facts for Kids
https://kids.kiddle.co/Women%27s_National_Basketball_Association

INDEX

Brondello, Sandy, 28

Charles, Tina, 17, 24

Hammon, Becky, 16

Ionescu, Sabrina, 5, 11, 18, 28

Jones, Jonquel, 12, 28

Statue of Liberty, 9

Stewart, Breanna, 5–6, 12, 18–19, 25, 28

Vandersloot, Courtney, 5–6, 12, 28

Weatherspoon, Teresa, 5, 10, 12, 15–16, 22–23

WNBA Draft, 5, 11, 16, 18

WNBA Finals, 5, 10–11, 15, 18, 21

PHOTO ACKNOWLEDGMENTS

Image credits: Erica Denhoff/Icon Sportswire/Getty Images, p.4; M. Anthony Nesmith/Icon Sportswire/Getty Images, p.6; Erica Denhoff/Icon Sportswire/Getty Images, p.7; Bruce Bennett/Getty Images Sport/Getty Images, p.8; Duncan Williams/Icon Sportswire/Getty Images, p.9; Todd Warshaw/Allsport/Getty Images, p.10; Luke Hales/Getty Images Sport/Getty Images, p.11; Dustin Satloff/Getty Images Sport/Getty Images, p.12; Craig Jones/Allsport/Getty Images, p.13; Ethan Miller/Getty Images Sport/Getty Images, p.14; Doug Pensinger/Allsport/Getty Images, p.15; Otto Greule Jr./Allsport/Getty Images, p.16; John Jones/Icon Sportswire/Getty Images, p.17; Stacy Revere/Getty Images Sport/Getty Images, p.18; Sarah Stier/Getty Images Sport/Getty Images, p.19; Ezra Shaw/Allsport/Getty Images, p.20; H.R.Celestin/UPI Photo Service/Newscom, p.21; Todd Warshaw/Allsport/Getty Images, p.22; Todd Warshaw/Allsport/Getty Images, p.23; Leon Bennett/Getty Images Sport/Getty Images, p.24; Bruce Bennett/Getty Images Sport/Getty Images, p.25; Bruce Bennett/Getty Images Sport/Getty Images, p.26; Luke Hales/Getty Images Sport/Getty Images, p.27; Erica Denhoff/Icon Sportswire/Getty Images, p.28; Luke Hales/Getty Images Sport/Getty Images, p.29

Cover image: Dylan Buell/Getty Images Sport/Getty Images